Living Words for The Soul

By Kurtis "B.O.K" Palacios

2

Hello,

I am B.O.K, I'm the higher self of Kurtis Palacios and I would love to give a warm thank you for listening to your intuition and following the guidance to be where you are now. All the inner work you're doing is paying off and is needed in order for our world to be a better place. All of heaven is within us and by embracing the divine spark we further the expansion of the cosmic energy that wishes to manifest on Earth! Isn't this such an exciting time to be alive☺. "Living Words for The Soul" is a collection of empowering poetic prayers that speak in first person affirmation form. With the intention to spark in-sight, inspiration and tap into the universal source of creation to set in motion the manifest our true authentic self! This book is great to meditate with and read before and after sleep. Allow your intuition to guide your eye to which poem will be read. To get the most out of this book, feel the words and allow your mind's eye to flourish in the boundless sea of imagination.

Again, thank you for being who you are and taking the steps to become the expression of the Divine Spark you are! You are love, and loved, infinity by the source that lives in all things. May this book bless you with peace, clarity and in-sight to the truth of your existence, thank you. ☺ Now, let's take three deep breaths with your eyes open or closed. Be mindful of your breath and bring your focus into your heart space. That's it. Relax.

Let your body loosen….. Good☺

Shining Heart

In this moment I am aware of the in dwelling presence of the infinite wisdom and power that has always been within me. I am intimately connected and inspired by this internal presence that connects me to the deepest aspects of my being. I find the strength and courage within me to live the life of my dreams. I am grateful for the awareness of this internal presence. I allow my heart to shine as I journey with my soul's highest purpose. Knowing I'm always in the right place at the time. I am grateful for this realization and I walk forth with the sun in my heart. I release these words to the Divine Source of Intelligence believing now, this is so.

Thank you.

Receiving and Transmitting

As my heart pumps to keep me alive, not only is it sending blood through the highway system of my blood stream. It's also a transmitter and receiver of subtle energies moving throughout the divine field of intelligence. Creating a non-locality effect which means there's no separation between here and there and any moment of time. Studies have shown in the book "The Heart's Code" our heart is literally, a mind of its own. Our heart is made up of trillions of memory cells, acting as pathways that link us with the heart of the universe. This is what makes me one with the horizon; via the metaphysical web that binds everything together. I Experience this moment in time as a example of consciousness experiencing itself. With a deep breath….I embrace the whispers of the warm sensations of my being, knowing, I am in alignment with the butterfly effect of the flower of life.

I am one with the Horizon and beyond.

Higher Presence

I recognize there is a higher presence of reality. I am in tune with this higher presence. As I meditate, I embrace my divine spirit and my soul purpose becomes clearer and clearer. As I walk my sacred path I am free and see all the opportunities that serve me. Focusing my attention on that which makes me laugh, smile and live more fully! With a deep breath.......... I embody all that I am. I recognize all the love and inner peace which leads to clarity. The clarity that's always been within me, I am eternally growing and showing my true colors as I internally become more aware of the expression that lives through me! With a heart full of gratitude, I accept this realization and let go, and allow God. Knowing with full faith within me and the wealth of the universal winds will provide the people and information I'll need to succeed in the chosen path my heart resonates with. I accept the responsibility of taking action on my ideas and living the life of my authentic self! Thank you Great Spirit as I feel this to be true.

I am blessed and guided.

Creative Living

Our mind's eye enables us to see beyond the physical world, and into the sight of spirit. I spiritually perceive the world through my mind's eye. Decalcified and open, I am gifted with the ability to see clairvoyantly and live in alignment with the full potential of my hearts passion! With clarity of who I am, and the expression I love to give, I am able to see and feel the life I came here to live. Attracting the reflection of my presence, I give thanks to those who come into my life with similar intentions. I consistently take action towards growing into the person I envision myself being. I resonate the feeling of the life I am, in my body, mind and heart and crystalize the subatomic particles within the etheric realm of life! Knowing in this moment this experience is real and that I am the life of my reality! In this moment now and forever into the future I create my destiny. I give thanks and appreciation to the Great Spirit of divine intelligence for listening, feeling and envisioning this reality with me. I ask for the guidance, courage and strength to be who I am. Thank you God, and so I am.

I am The Life of the Dream.

The Horizon

I am internally connected to the horizon and beyond. As I breath and embrace all that I am, I find the eternal land of breathing trees and voluptuous ocean seas. Moving with divine timing and aligning with synchronicities. The infinite thought wave perceives life through me as I am gifted to enjoy creating with this eternal stream. Reflecting the horizon from the serene space of my heart centered mission. Lifting the vibration by connecting with God's infinite life source, then stopping to listen. I receive guidance in ways that are most conspicuous. I am confident in the expression of my craft and within the space of my heart, I experience the connection to everything which I effect through my positive intention. Through positive intention my life changes as I see and believe it to be. Like karate chopping wood my intention creates my destiny. With a smile in my heart, I fully accept myself as successful, now! Immediately, I attract that which is in harmony with the intention of my heart's desire. I walk forward knowing I am blessed and supported by the heart of the universe. Thank you Great Spirit, and so this is.

The vibration of my intention is harmonized by the Universe.

Forever Expanding

Inside me is an ever expanding life force that grows and creates as I think and feel. Feeling the subtle energy of the shifting seasons, I am guided and intuitively know, what is in resonance with my higher self. I am in tune with the current of life. I am aware of the signs and synchronicities that guide me to make the choices and decisions that will lead to the highest good and overall wellbeing. I am grateful; I am aware and open to the immeasurable life force that breath's, dances, grows and creates through me. I create a difference in the world by simply being myself. The true beauty within me lives in the midst of eternity. So I paint my life in harmony with who I am. Thank you Universe for listening as I know I am guided by your grace.

Thank you. And so it is.

Life is simply how we like to play!

Limitless in the Moment

My body ages as my soul remains wise. Forever connected to the moment. I am growing and showing myself new heights as I expanded as the sky. I can see the prize within my mind's eye. I visualize that which is already am, seeing truth and being truth where ever my vista lands. I create a domino effect that effectively changes where ever I stand; as I grow into the highest evolution of consciousness being myself. I serve the world by being this radiant self. Happy and open I am guided by love. So I pray to God, spirit, source that our lives are filled with joy, balance, love, fun and dancing lol. Positive energy, with abundance to share and more than enough resources, time and energy for the well-being of ourselves and families. Being the divine channel I am, I release these words with great gratitude to the Divine Source of Intelligence. Knowing, that which I ask is received. Thank you Great Spirit and so this is.

I am a Magnet of Divine Grace.

Gaining Perspective

I aspire to teach, learn and grow as an individual. By learning more about who I am and how to just be, I learn more about myself and I learn more about others as well. I learn how to appreciating myself more, and how I can appreciate everyone else for who they are as well. Finding and looking at the beauty in life, I find it within myself and within other people too. I know I am beautiful. From the inside out, life expresses its self through me. Like light shining through a clear glass pyramid, I am a reflection of life and I have a choice in how I want to respond to situations that are outside of my control. As I know, life is just going to happen. So by letting go of judgment of how I "think life should be." I let go of that which I cannot control and I detach from the situation, and see objectively what this situation is teaching me. Like placing it in a snow globe I gain perspective and grow from where I am at in this moment and look forward, with a new awareness of myself. Because I am a reflection of life, and life is a reflection of me. From within to without, I learn, grow and teach by my example. I am the student and master of my life.

I am a servant of the silence

Let's see where this goes

(Meditation)

I invite us to take 3 deep breaths, releasing with each exhale and relaxing with each inhale. Starting from birth visualize everything that's happen to you in order for you to be here now. Where have I been, who have I been and who have I surrounded myself with? What story am I telling?? What roll am I playing? Why? (Keep in mind, the spark has always been with us;) Where do we go from here? :) What have I learned? What's my next step? What resonates with my heart?

Love gate

The fabric of the universe in which the core essence of my being exist in, is love. The harmony of the universe play's through my soul and throughout the galaxies of time and space. I am the bridge between nothing and everything in a moment of time. I am the proof of how harmonious the timing is, in which the universe plays through me. It's been a trip yet I've come so far to be where I am in this moment now. Life will continue to show me the beauty it bestows upon those who listen to that which has always been present. With a deep breath... I Feel one with how connected I am with the ages. I naturally start living with the timing of the song the universe sings through me. I am one with this source of harmony and I allow the song of my

heart to be felt throughout the days.
Thank you.

I am a cosmic love gate

I am

I am history and I am the future. Yet I am this present moment right now. Who am I? I am a part of the sky and as light as the clouds drifting by. You see that head lamp, I am that head lamp. As bright as the full moon lighting up the night sky, I am that I am. Like every bird you see to every crashing wave. I am the warm sun, shining on your face. I am that I am. I am a bunny, a whale and I am also a kitty. I am the love in your heart and likewise your love is within me. The beautiful pictures you paint, I am within thy painting.

Love letter from God.

Success

Success is who I am and revolves around being the expression that lives through me. The truest expression in which is creative, fun and happy, lives within me and is relevant in all areas of my life! Every person is successful at becoming something. The true beauty is blooming into the life we came here to be. Expanding our authentic ability to express the craft, gifts, and skills that makes us feel most alive! In this sense I will keep growing and thrive! I evolve like the blooming effect of spring. Attracting Hummingbirds and bee's so the nectar of my true self-reflection nourishes those who seek their true self-expression.

I am Successful being myself

Being Myself

A Sacred sight as I stare into my eyes. With a state of being that lives within the essence of time. I am a wise soul who lives in the knowing of eternity. What I see is only the tip of the ice berg. What I feel, is like diving off the edge and splashing into the depths of an infinite ocean. An ocean that lives with conscious awareness. An ocean that encompasses all life. I sing like the whales and play humbly like dolphins. Telepathically communicate a radiant feeling of my true presence. I creatively uplift my environment by simply being a channel. Flowing and swimming through the essence of time. I find myself experiencing deeper level of awareness where the present moment is all there is. I am Peace on earth. With great gratitude I thank my mother giving birth to me. Allowing the chance for me to experience this moment on Earth. Through my example I share the most beautiful blessing of all. Myself.☺

Thanks Mom☺

A Miracle within its Self

The essence of my spirit is connected to everything. I am a miracle experiencing its self in human form; a vibration uniquely expressing its individuality. I'm so young and yet I'm so old. My soul creates ripples with each thought, prayer and word I speak. I am Responsible for the creation of my reality. So I make sure I am integrity and live with honesty because I know in my heart, the soul of the universe conspires to help me. So the more honest I am with myself, the more truth is spread throughout the world.

Giving thanks for my blessings and counting them so that way I am aware, of all the people who love me and aware of all the miracles that happen throughout the day. Thank you God, for blessing me with life.

I am the source of happiness.

Grateful

I'm grateful for life. I'm grateful to be love and to be loved by life itself. I'm grateful for the growing pains and the lessons they've taught me. I'm grateful to be connected to the divine spark within me and the blessings it bestows upon me and others. I'm grateful for the time I have to grow into the person I am. I take the time to listen to the silent space of the divine within me. Providing for my every need and supporting me, in its most mysterious ways. I'm grateful to be aligned with who I am and strive to live authentically every day. I'm grateful for my wonderful friends and their beautiful reflection shining right back to me, because who I am, is a beautiful blessing that lives on forever.

I am Legend

A Dreaming Gift

I feel the hum of the magnetic force of my being as I create and manifest my intentions, attracting that which is like my intention. As I feel my authentic resonance, my actions and decisions become clearer. I connect and harmonize with source, and feel my wildest dreams as real in this now moment. (Deep Breath) Feeling myself becoming lighter and brighter, I know I am growing into the highest version of who I am. I am like a fire igniting the path to a palace in the sky. The life I feel in my heart is the refection of the heart of the universe. I am the nature of the universe in which I live in. I am a gift dreaming reality into existence on two legs within a suit of skin.

It's Exciting to know I am the expression of the life I envision.

Infinite Potential

Within the essence of the universe live the possibilities of all potential experiences. The projection I choose to see is the experience I attract and live today. Like clay I mold my day. A positive attitude goes a long way. Attracting the reflection which leads me to see the people, environments and situations that harmonize with what I'm putting out. I positively affect the world around me, by loving myself. Coming from love, I attract the frequency of love within a holographic universe. From this point of compassion and self-care I create a space where I attract the most loving potentialities. Within this space exists abundance and prosperity in all possibilities.

Anything is Possibilities!

Fountain of Life

Moment by moment, I am becoming wiser and more adapted to the universal intelligence livin through me, as me, and being the God spark I came here to be. I am a creator of my reality and move forth with the awareness to recognize opportunities that serve the manifestation of my highest good. This helps me and the world at large by living life as my authentic self. I am the change I want to see. Like a fountain flowing into the unknown, I expect the unexpected. Boldly living out of the box where eagles fly. My instincts and inner wisdom guides my eye. I see what I want from afar and glide towards the direction of my prize. As I sway with the wind from side to side. Never losing sight of the prize with knowingness the prize is already mine.

I focus on my goals and they happen.

Lifetime of Thanks

I am thankful my healthy mind, body and spirit keep me thriving towards my goals. I am supported and energized by a divine intelligence that exists within me and the sky. Forever supporting me to succeed in how ever I envision myself being. Grateful to be alive in such changing times, I strive to be the best I can be every day in every way, knowing my path lights up for me coming from an authentic place. Present in this moment, I consistently grow into my highest potential; I reach my goals, step by step. I sit and meditate to reconnect, rebalance and to clarify my next steps. Guided by my heart I am grateful for this human experience. I am grateful for this brand new day and the opportunity it brings to create the life I came here to live. I am thankful for the presence of this universal source for blessing me with a healthy body, mind and strong spirit. I am blessed and honored to practice seeing God in myself, everyone, and everything. The language of the universe speaks to me as I practice. With an open heart, filled with love and appreciation, I release my gratitude to the cosmos. Believing whole heartedly, the life I envision is orchestrating its self into my reality with every action step towards my vision. Thank you God for listening, and so it is.

Timeless and Immortal

I've come to grips that one day I will leave this physical experience behind and look back on how I loved and shared the gifts of my soul. Bringing with me a lifetime of wisdom and a familiar feeling when I read these words again. Somehow in some way this moment will last forever. Maybe when we transition we'll understand, and then forget all over again so we can experience more life and live fully in this moment. Knowing this moment is forever present, I experience life to its fullest now! I no long wait for the right time or situation to happen in order for me to live my dreams. I do what I can Now, today, with belief and trust that inevitably the reality of my dream is waiting for me. (Deep Breath) I am worthy to receive this reality as my life because it is why I am here on this planet! I am flexible in how this reality takes form and focus on loving myself and appreciating where I'm at, now. (Deep Breath) I am unique, talented, and clever enough to manifest my dreams. I'm grateful for the signs and set small goals to reach my ultimate goals. My thoughts become things and these thing attract to me.

The strength of my belief makes my dreams appear.

The Formless Spirit

I was once the ocean, encompassing all life, energy, stars and stillness. I then eroded the Earth and stones that wished to drink life. As I granted the Earth's wish she began to form sand. I too became the sand. With each grain having a purpose to serve to make up the beach; the beach then came to life. I rose from the sand, not truly aware of the power that existed in me. Life was a struggle, trying to evolve forward. "I was once part of the ocean with full awareness of the immense strength, power, and connectedness with the star's I'm innately a part of. Wait, I am apart of…. So I am the sand as well. Like the star's I shine, even as sand." Realizing this I crystalized and became man. Like a light house with consciousness beaming from my eyes. I felt a warm tingle as calm as the morning mist. Looking around, I realize now I am the creation of all this. All that I see, and all that I am. I am the ocean and I am the sand.

-The Formless Spirit

The Dawn of a New Perspective

Twinkle Twinkle little stars. So close and so far, Mother Earth gazed in amazement. Young in galactic years and yet, very beautiful. It's like she barley 18. Awake and wise she sees between the lines. No longer is she allowing herself to be abused by corrupted minds. So she ask father God, "May I receive more Light, Insight, and Divine Healing?" The doorbell rang and here we came. The Warriors of the light here to opening the door for Mother Earth to change. The door of light, the door of love and the door of truth. Mother Earth went inside and said, "Oh My God, I love it in here. I am galacticly connected to more than just the twinkling stars. I bring harmony to galaxies' far beyond from what I have ever known. Mother Earth then closed her eyes and became still, allowing her heart to glow. Like the morning sun rise it Dawn on her, "I am the Divine Healing I've asked for. My heart is the source to galactic connection. I am awake to the cosmic perspective." As she affirmed this her cells started to regenerate. Becoming lighter and brighter, she began to create a reality of true harmony and peace by manifest her highest goals and dreams. Losing the monetary system, and creating multiple ways of utilizing the abundance of free energy resources. Using hemp instead of plastic, cars propelled by magnates. Food that's organic and music that leaves us feel fantastic. It's all possible if we dare to imagine.

-The Dawn of a New Perspective

Intuitive Trust

The ocean of change is always moving and is fulfilling when we embrace the flow and surf the waves of change. Like the goose bumps I feel when I listen to that song I needed to hear. The more I recognize the unity of God's grace in all, the more I understand the language and signs of divine synchronicities. I trust my intuition and I trust in my ability to be the change I want to see in the world. By tuning into the frequency of the natural state of spirit, I positively affect my environment and raise the frequency of the planet. Who I am is plenty, my essence affects many. Balanced within silence I receive guidance to my prayers. I know within my soul I have the courage to apply the information I am always receiving. I believe in my heart, I have what it

takes to create heaven on Earth. The an-
swers within me create New Earth.

I trust my intuition.

Moving Through Me

We do things because we like to do'em.
If not, then what are we doing? It's easy
to get caught in the fog but the sun in-
side makes it quite clear to see the direc-
tion we are passionate about. So who's
to say I should be this way or that way. I
live my life in the direction that feels best
in alignment with my heart and soul. Al-
lowing myself to flow; creates outcomes
totally unexpected. Creating movement
and movements because, it, moves
through us. So I trust my gut and listen
closely because life is moving through
me.

Energy flows where my focus goes

MY SHADOW

I've made mistakes; I've lied, cheated and stolen. I've used people for my selfish intentions but it's from these actions; I see how I can respond to the actions of my shadow. Recognizing and accepting; Yes, I have done these actions and I immediately become present and have the chance to look at myself from a different perspective and say, "I forgive you. I forgive myself and love and accept myself fully." Taking a deep breath in, to connect with myself (BREATH) and know.

It's okay☺

I AM alive, and I have the chance to recreate my life in this present moment. Just by the way I look at this particular situation. I'm not perfect but I accept my imperfections and with that, it's my imperfections that make me perfect. I choose to be honest with myself and with everyone around me. I am transforming my world into my inner reality. My inner reality creates the formality of our Physical experience. The third dimension is the greatest invention. Envisioning the life we imagine ourselves living.

Thank you and B.O.K

In this Moment

(Higher Self Connection)

In this Moment...

Our planet spins; the sun shines its rays upon Earths beautiful face. Shooting stars are being born in human form and also returning back to where ever the soul came from.

In this Moment....

Manifestations are taking form and the entire world is changing and shifting from each individual raising their frequency and awareness. Morphing into the perspective of a collective mind of humanity. I positively influence the world by starting with me and taking responsibility of my thoughts, beliefs and feelings! So... as I connect and feel the

intimacy of the relation I have with eve-
rything around me and within me. I find
myself, and how I influence the world by
simply living from this internal state of
love. I realize the perception of how I see
myself, creates an effect that's equiva-
lent to the explosion of a star giving birth
to new life! Humanity is reborn. I am re-
born.

In this Moment.

(Deep Breath)

Across the Bridge

Deep down a frown can be a bridge to a new beginning that's waiting to be acknowledged. With each step I take across this bridge, this frown turns into a smile while I uncover and let go of all the baggage I've held onto. Breathing into this space and knowing I am ok. The core of who I am is always ok. I leave what was behind and I embrace the journey of life and choose to live in the moment and to my fullest potential! Light emanates from my heart, and with each breath I allow this light to expand! Filling each chakra and clearing each ethereal body I am. Knowing I Am consciousness, I Am Beautiful, Genius, Intuitive and intelligent. I am grateful to be this bright sunshiny day.

I am a Sunshiny Day.

In this Moment

I recognize the presence of god in this moment. Breathing the awareness of all that I am; I am sacred, intelligent and wise. Creating a space infused with love, new worlds are created in the blink of an eye and the whispers of Angelic wisdom surround me. Safe in this knowing, my heart merges with oneness and the galactic truth of my spirit. I internally cleanse myself through diet, exercise, and mediation. Creating and cultivating my inner world I awaken to the dream that I am, and I embrace thyself as a creator. Creating a world that resonates with the divine spark within me. I am open to divine healing energy, sacred wisdom and guidance. Thank you source of creation for all that I am and bestowing the bless of your grace through me.

I am Divine channel of healing.

Portal within Creation

Heart connection is the blessing merging Heaven and Earth. By feeling the love of my inner child, I am born into the awareness of my spiritual nature. Having compassion of the light inside me reveals a Vesica Pisces portal into a land of infinite possibility. Consciousness is the kingdom of heaven, merging 7 chakras into 1, body of consciousness. I flow with creative energy knowing I am a body of consciousness. Shining like the sun because the truth of who I am is warm, open, and promotes life! I allow myself to be open to my greatest potential. Knowing I always prevail when I let go and let God. Today, I allow myself to let go and have fun.

And so I am☺

The light Behind the Dots.

I describe reality imaginatively. Creating a fun world that lives in fantasy. Like the realm of spirit connecting the dots and lovingly placing a picture in front of light. So life can reflect itself through my eyes and I can realize myself in human form. I uniquely express myself to create harmony within the heart of mankind. So I let go of what was taught in the past to learn more about the soul of the universe. I embrace and remember the soul's beauty, strength and Spiderman-like abilities to sense when energy is in motion. A tribal instinct that's growing more roots as humanity begins to feel more and think more fruitfully. I create whole worlds in just a blink of an eye. I live tomorrow's ancient past today, as I sink into the present moment.

I am heaven on Earth.

Young Body, Wise Soul

Believers dream reality and live to be their fantasy, in spite of society's old way of thought. I embrace the spark within me and expand the light beyond my body. I am the example of an enlightened soul! Continuously choosing to learn and keep moving forward! Because within me is a gift so unique to who I am, it is my responsibility to develop it and share it with the world. I fly on the wings of belief that the universe is creating with each thought I think. Trusting the process and trusting in who I am, with 100% reassurance my dreams are real and are manifesting right now! I am the focal point of Heaven on earth and my heart is the gateway within the kingdom. I am young, yet old. I am wise, yet I have the chance to learn more about who I am as life unfold into another chapter.

Life lives as I do.

Bed of Flowers

"I believe in myself and I believe in you." Whispered the heart. I am disciplined in growing the light within my life. My body is a bed of flowers blooming from the joy of infinity. As laid back as a cloud, I flow in the stream of consciousness. Sparkling like star dust, the nectar of my being attracts hummingbirds and bees. Spreading liveliness everywhere I go! Humbly rooted into the present moment, I am hydrated by the conscious stream of life. Protected and provided for as I listen to the guidance of my intuition. I am lead throughout the course of this lifetime by the subtleties of life. (Deep Breath) With great gratitude I'm thankful for all the synchronicities throughout my life journey for making it possible for me to experience the blooming effect

of life's mysterious ways. Thank you God
as I let go and allow the heart to open
and listen to your mysterious ways.

I am guided by intelligence.

Flow in my Life

I am ready to receive more flow in my life. With life consistently changing, it gives me infinite amounts of options to new adventures and to attract more of what I want. By practicing self-love first, I begin to reshape my life experience starting from where I am right now!:) So who am I? What excites me the most? How can I contribute that, which excites me the most, to my everyday life? As I listen, the answers will come. Ask and I shall receive, search and I shall find and as I believe so it shall be. With a deep breath (Deep Breath) I relax my mind and my body. I am now my breath and sink into this present moment.

The purpose of life is right here. Thank you☺

The Depth of Connection

I remember the depth of connection I am. The power of love that emanates from the center of my being guides my life by simply letting go. Letting go of all my worries and the rolls people try to tell me to play and listen to myself, because who I am, is like no other. I am special and unique and it gives me goose bumps and a calm state of mind feeling the essence of my being. I practice speaking my truth and stand up for what I believe in today. Today, I create a life in harmony with who I am. The depth of connection exude through every pore of my body and go beyond what the mind can fathom and can only be felt by soul. I allow myself to open more and more like a lotus flower blooming from the mud to the sun.

One by one we inspire the frequency to rise! I am consciousness swelling and telling the stories of tomorrow by experiencing the depths of the soul today.

I am the nature of the universe that lives through me.

Correct Thinking

With a deep breath in (Breath Deeply) I sink into the moment of the divine self and observing the circuitry of how my thoughts flow. Throughout the day I allow my thoughts to go, with no judgment, being the observer, I become mindfully aware of the essence of my thoughts. Breathing into the breath of life I become still, I awaken to my *Self*; a cosmic state of being, as I listen to the silence of my soul. From the state of oneness, life becomes a warm web of connection that shines like the reflection of the sun, shimmering off the ocean. Reborn as I walk forth in this state of love, trusting and open to God's Divine intelligence and the fact that the universe and I are no different. I am abundant, miraculous and beautiful, just as I am. *"Listen to your heart." whispered the universe.*

I Am That I Am.

I am Life

I am Life; I am surrounded by love and by people who love me for who I am. I am cherished and welcomed with smiles and excitement. I am confident and delighted to express my passion. With a warm smile in my heart and eyes, people can feel the warmth of my love radiating from me like warm mist. Relaxed and at ease I am grounded, centered and fun to be around and firm when I need to be. Balanced and happy, I relax and allow the manifestation of my soul's intention to unfold. Poem by poem, thought by thought the butterfly effect of my actions and decisions live forever. I am the seed life grows from! Today is a great day to create the future!

Today creates tomorrow.

Trust

Trust and have faith in yourself. Your intuitive sense is the best in the world. Inner wisdom flows from you! The answers are home so relax, and let go. Trust like you know the sun will rise. Kiss your worries goodbye and know everything is fine. A fantastic Infinite Notion Electrified is within your eyes. So take a deep breath, rest and close your eyes. I allow answers to flow from the subconscious mind. I am aware of the background voice and with this recognition, I now have the choice to choose and grow from here. I am right where I need to be in order to grow like a peach tree☺

Today, I practice trusting **_myself!_**

Transformation

As the seasons move, I take the time to recognize the beauty of the movement. Like music in motion, my wishes are confirmed in a synchronistic enfoldment of events. Living tomorrow today, (Deep Breath) I know, I am one with the eternal source that lives in a timeless way. I am grateful for all the positive people who surround me and see me for who I am. With an eternal smile, I am grounded and I allow this energy to flow through me as I embrace the feeling of being nurtured. Visualizing myself as healed from a cellular level, I reflect my reflection and heal the planet starring with me. I am healthy, balanced and transformed. (DEEP BREATH) "Thank you Great Spirit as I embrace transformation." Said mother Earth;)

Creation of Harmony

As I breath I am instantly reminded of
the vastness I am apart of.
A sense of belonging and joy, open's up
to me as I open up to the essence of who
I am. Transparent and light, happy know-
ing I've uncovered the layers of dogma
to get to the root core of my existence. I
am a creation and extension of God.
Open and eternally connected to... eve-
rything and everyone. I am always found
as I allow and accept myself for who I
am. Starting from the inside out I create
my world and collaborate with everyone
around me to make a better world! I am
the group; I am the environment and
within the open state of presence and
expansion exists the miracle of giving,
creating, and elevating everyone and
everything. I sense this feeling now, and
allow the presence of this miracle to fill
me, heal me, to live through me and
guide me through all I experience in this
life. I am grateful for

this experience and allow the creator to guide my life, now. I am grateful for the source of creation for living through me and expressing its beauty, love, and harmony as me. As I am so is everyone else and so it is.

I collaborate with everything to make a better world.

Positive Effect

As I watch the grace of the breeze blow, I know my thoughts go with it. Connecting to the quiet place within me, I feel the positivity I am. From this place is the movement of dance. A chance to express the feeling of life! I creatively use this silence to see the reality that best resonates with my soul. Feeling the ring of the warm song my heart sings. I am guided as the Universe Conspires to help me. With this understanding, I am grateful to give the expression of the positive energy I am. As I let this feeling ripple through the field of divine intelligence, I know I will receive that which is of the same vibrational essence. With great gratitude I accept this now. Thank you God and so it is.

Perfection in God's Grace

I am filled with God's grace. I am blessed in the grace of all that I am. Knowing who I am, I am truly grateful to remember the strength, beauty and power that exist within my soul. One with the elements, I remember I am apart of the creation of all that I see. I express, share and bless the world, with the authentic expression of my soul. By accepting my divine expression, I let go of judgment of what it means to be myself and I grow into the expression of Gods image. Imperfect yet, perfect in the fluid dance of life. In the image of God, I am perfect. In the image of God, I see myself. Thank you Great Spirit, for this life I live.

You are Amazing and worthy to receive all the blessings, Love, and abundance attracted to you in this moment now. Thank you; and God bless.

"Enjoy every second of life,

because every second, is a lifetime to remember."-Kurtis Palacios

Kurtis Palacios, an old soul in a young body, who's been writing poetry for ages. In this life time he started writing poetry when he was 12 years of age. Inspired by 2pac. Kurtis knew he had discovered something special within himself. so at the age of 12 he began writing stories, poems and song. As he developed a flow for writing, he graduated to the art of rhythmic poetic freestyle speech, and public speaking. Combining the expressions, he used this art form to empower himself and others around him. Kurtis began to realize the effect his words had on people and started using his poetry to paint universal truths and express the gifts of his soul. This has led to the creation of "Living Words for The Soul." Kurtis is now a public speaker and sound healing therapist who travels the world sharing his words, music and life experience to bring the world together with honesty and authenticity. To learn more about Kurtis go to KurtisPalacios.com

Thank you for listening to your intuition;)